#

Anne & Harlow Rockwell

A Harper Trophy Book

Harper & Row, Publishers

for Oliver

Machines work.

We use

machines.

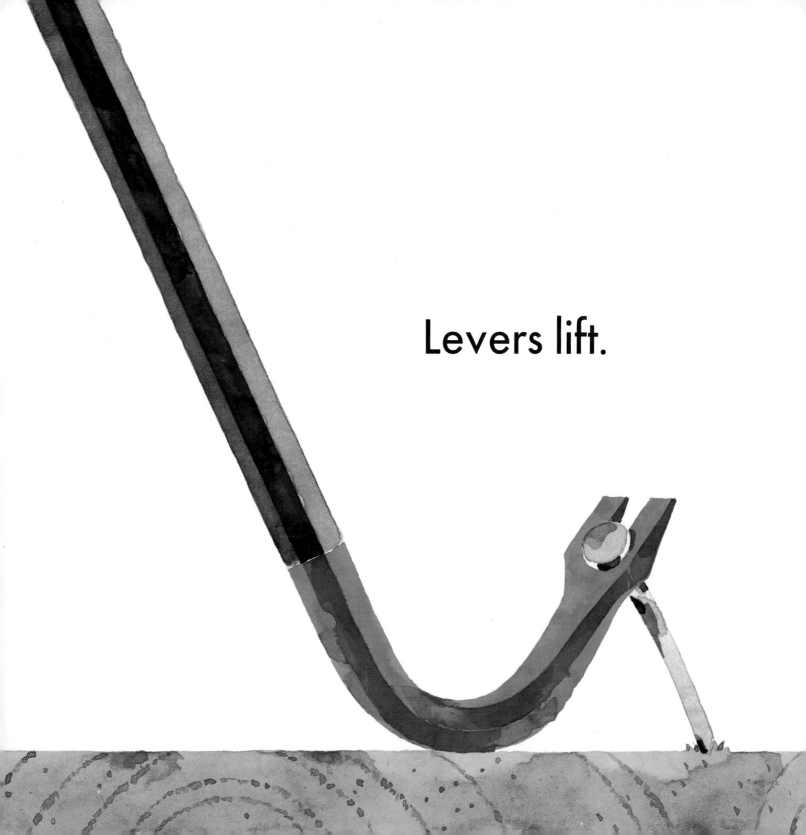

Levers lift.

Wheels turn.

A pulley is a wheel
with a groove
for a rope.

A block and tackle
to pull things up
is made of pulleys.

A gear is a wheel with teeth
that turn another gear.

Ball bearings make wheels
turn smoothly.

A jackscrew raises heavy things.

Sprockets on a wheel
grip holes in a chain.
They pull the chain
around and around.

Fuel makes some

machines work.

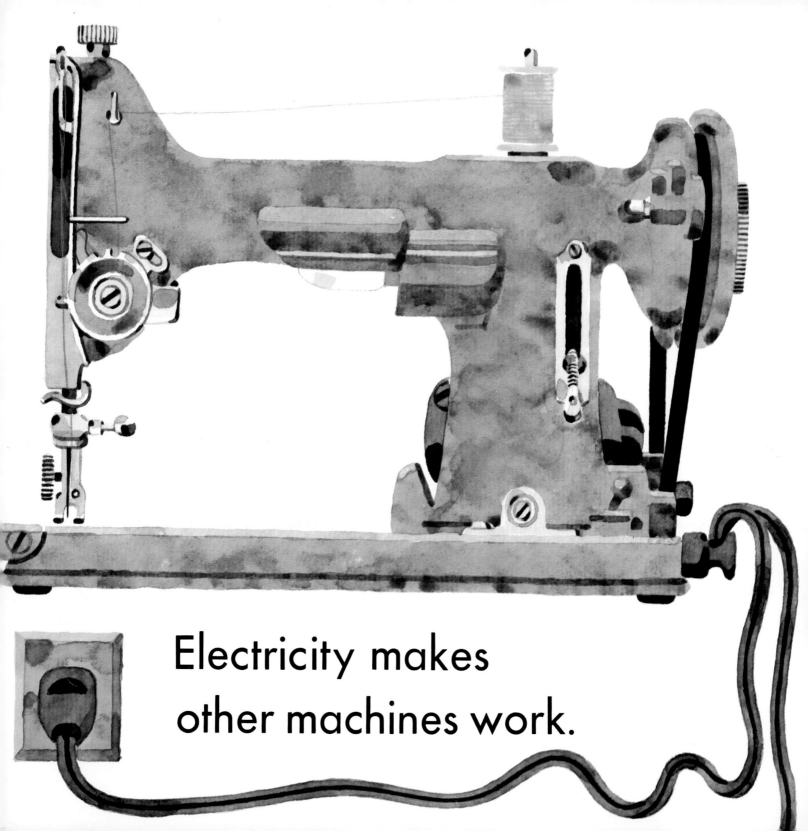

Electricity makes
other machines work.

Hands make others work.

My bicycle is a machine.
My feet make it work.

There are many machines
that do many things.

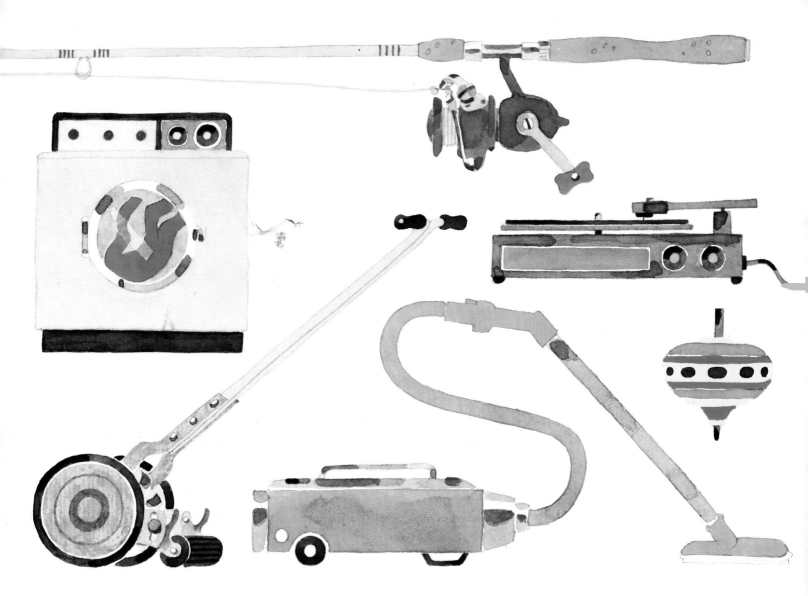

I like machines.